D0865534

le of Contents

You and Your Mouse

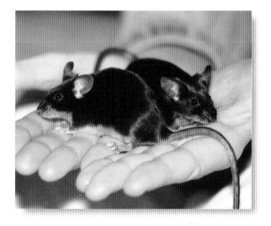

Congratulations on your decision to bring home a mouse. A mouse can be a delightful and friendly little pet. Mice are perky, energetic animals who will amuse you with their antics.

The species kept as a pet, the house mouse (*Mus musculus*), has a long history with people. Although mice were initially viewed as pests, because of the damage they inflicted on stored food and grain, people do have a soft spot for them. They are often seen as endearing, shy, and timid creatures.

Mice are tolerant of gentle handling, but they are too tiny to be truly cuddly pets.

The house mouse has been selectively bred in captivity for more than a century. The National Mouse Club of Great Britain was formed in 1895, giving mice a lineage that can be compared with that of dogs, cats, and rabbits.

Mice as Pets

Not counting their tail, mice measure less than four inches in length. Their small size appeals to adults and children who are

Not Cuddlers

Mice can be friendly and can learn that seeing their owner means food and playtime. Some tame mice will even come to their cage door to greet their owner. However, mice are not cuddly pets. They do not mind being petted, but they prefer to crawl around and investigate their surroundings rather than being cuddled for long periods of time. Pet mice typically bite only when they are afraid or threatened, but they are not aggressive animals. Gentle, regular handling will make your pet docile and reduce the likelihood of him ever biting you.

captivated by the mouse's cute appearance. Mice are inexpensive, undemanding, and easy to care for. They can be kept in their cage full-time as long as they have a spacious and entertaining (toy-filled) cage in which to play. They can be as relaxing to watch as an aquarium of tropical fish. Mice can even remain unattended in their cage over the weekend as long as they are given extra food and water.

A pet mouse is very clean and performs an elaborate grooming ritual several times a day. The mouse first licks his front feet, then, using both front feet, he washes his face and behind his ears. Using his hind foot, the mouse delicately cleans the inside of his ears and then nibbles his toes clean. He continues washing the fur all over his body and then licks his hind toes after scratching with them. You will also see your pet mouse clean his long tail. Mice are extremely fastidious, and many even setup a separate toilet area in their cage.

Lifespan

Mice live between one and a half to three years. A short lifespan can be sad for pet owners who become attached to their mouse. The one advantage, however, of the short lifespan is that mice do not live so long that children become uninterested in them. Longer-lived pets, such as rabbits, can be neglected by children or their adult owners

These three-week-old mice are too young to be sold. Purchase mice that are at least five weeks old.

Mice are fastidious animals and will groom themselves several times daily.

once the novelty of owning the pet has worn off. Before you bring home a mouse, be sure that you are willing to commit to caring for your new pet for the rest of his lifetime.

How Many?

Although a mouse can be kept by himself, mice are social animals, and a single mouse will be happier and more playful if he has a friend. Part of the fun of keeping pet mice is watching them wrestle and play as they take turns chasing each others around their cage. Two mice will groom each other, especially in hard-to-reach places (such as the neck and back), and curl up next to each other to sleep.

A mouse kept alone tends to be less active, sleeps more, and, therefore, is less happy and less interesting. If, for some reason, you are set on getting only one mouse, plan on having playtime with your pet several times a day.

Buy two young mice at the same time so they can grow up together. Two female mice get along best. Males will fight as they get older and often must be kept alone. It is possible, however, to successfully

Quick & Easy Mouse Care

keep male mice together if both are purchased as young littermates. They must be provided with a cage that is at least two feet in length and that has two separate nest boxes. If you choose a male and a female, they will produce babies every 20 to 36 days. Neutering the male, which must be performed by a qualified veterinarian, will prevent the male from impregnating the female.

Adult mice (about 12 weeks of age) are territorial and will fight if an unfamiliar mouse is placed into their home. If one of the pair dies, you can try to introduce a new mouse. An adult mouse will more readily accept a younger mouse but also may attack the newcomer. Introduce the new mouse by placing his cage next to the

Senses

Mice have some acute senses that help them to survive, but eyesight is not one of them. Mice have poor vision. They can detect little or no color, so they see in various shades of gray. Bright light can damage a mouse's eyes. Mice naturally avoid bright lights because they are nocturnal, which means they are active at night.

Mice have an acute sense of hearing. They can communicate and hear sounds in the ultrasonic range, which people cannot hear. For the first two weeks of their life, baby mice communicate with their parents using ultrasonic sounds. Mice make ultrasonic calls when mating and fighting, as well as high-pitched squaking sound that people can hear.

A keen sense of smell helps mice locate food and detect pheromones used in social interactions. Pheromones are chemicals secreted from the body that facilitate communication between members of the same species. An example of this is territorial urine-marking. Male mice, in particular, mark their territory with urine and droppings, so that other male mice, especially younger males, will avoid the marked area.

A mother mouse with her brood. Mice can start breeding when they are six to eight weeks old.

cage of the old pet for about a week before trying to add the new mouse to the existing cage.

Male or Female

Male mice are called bucks and females are called does. Male mice are larger than females and have a stronger "mousy" smell. Because male mice are smellier, many pet owners prefer female mice. The strong odor associated with male mice can be reduced by neutering. Although this can be a relatively expensive option compared with the initial purchase price of the mouse, it is money well spent if the only other option is to find a new home for a beloved pet because of a family member's complaints of odor.

Be aware that a female mouse may be pregnant if she was not separated from the males soon enough. Female mice can breed at six weeks of age and males can start breeding at six to eight weeks of age. A female mouse can give birth to up to 12 babies after a gestation period of 19 to 21 days. Baby mice are born pink and

Whiskers

Mice use their whiskers to help them navigate. The whiskers that are found near the eyes, lips, and cheeks greatly aid a mouse as he wanders. When a mouse is scampering about, the whiskers on his cheeks perceive the horizontal and ground surfaces, while the ones above his eyes detect overhead surfaces.

Teeth

A mouse has two pairs of chisel-like incisors in the front of his mouth. These teeth never stop growing. The incisors enable a mouse to carry nuts and other food items and to easily open hard seeds and nuts. A mouse's teeth are constantly worn down when he gnaws and chews on hard substances. If you look at a mouse's front teeth, you will notice that the lower incisors are up to three times longer than the upper incisors. Mice also have powerful jaw muscles and teeth. They can easily gnaw through the hard outer shell of a nut. The space between the incisors and the rear molars is called the diastema. When a mouse eats, his cheeks block this space to prevent any sharp food from being swallowed.

hairless, with their eyes closed, and they cannot be weaned from their mothers until they are at least three weeks old. Because of the possibility of a female being pregnant, buy your mice from a pet store that keeps the females and the males separately.

If you decide to keep a male and a female mouse together, and you do not have the male neutered, you can expect your pets to have babies for the duration of the female's reproductive life (which is

Baby mice begin life with their eyes closed and almost no hair. They are helpless and entirely dependent on their mother.

Mother mice are very defensive of their babies. If your mouse has babies, leave them alone as much as possible for the first few weeks.

about one and a half years). While this can be fun and interesting, do consider whether you can find new homes for all the babies your pets will be making. Pet stores might be interested in buying some of them, but they may not always need mice when you are trying to find new homes for your weaned mice.

Which Kind?

Decades of selective breeding have produced more than 50 color varieties of mice, and four coat types have been developed: satin,

Picking One Out

Mice are not really cuddly or loving pets, so do not expect to see your mouse run up to you, licking your face, and trying to snuggle up. However, the sign of a good mouse is one who will sit calmly but remain alert or climb around on his handler without any signs of fright or panic. This, then, is the mouse for you!

astrex, long-haired, and rex. Marked varieties include broken-marked nice, who have colored spots or patches distributed over a white background.

When fully grown, mice measure between four to six inches in body length. The have a slender pink tail that is almost as long as their body. Their tails are semi-prehensile and help them to climb.

Buying a Healthy Mouse

The premises of the pet store or breeder from where you buy your pet mice should be clean. Although some smell is normal, if the odor in the store or in the mice's cage is excessively pungent, buy your mice somewhere else. Check to be sure that the mice have enough food and clean water. And empty food dish and a dirty water bottle are signs of poor care, and mice housed in these conditions are less likely to be healthy.

A healthy mouse should have dense, shiny fur. The coat should be smooth and sleek with no bald spots or flaky skin. The mouse's eyes should be bold, bright, and clear. Choose a mouse who looks solid

Healthy mice have bright eyes, a neat and shiny coat, and a straight tail. They should also be alert and curious.

and is a little plump. A healthy mouse should not have an easily detected protruding backbone. Do not choose a mouse who is listless, sneezes, has runny eyes or a runny nose, a rough or thin coat, lumps, or scabs. Dirty, matted fur near a mouse's tail could be a sign of diarrhea.

Choose your mouse from a clean, uncrowded cage. Mice living in a dirty, crowded environment are less likely to be healthy. If any of the mice in a cage show symptoms of ill health, do not buy a mouse—no matter how much you may like a particular mouse or want to buy a pet mouse that day. The mouse you want may appear healthy, but he has been exposed to sick mice and is likely to become ill later (often triggered by the stress of going to a new home). The staff at the pet store or the breeder should be able to answer any questions you have about mice and their care.

A healthy mouse is curious and active. A good choice is a mouse who is inquisitive and investigates your hand when you place it in the cage. A mouse that sniffs your hand and runs away and then returns to further investigate you will also be a good pet. Do not choose a mouse who runs and hides, struggles frantically, or is aggressive and tries to bite.

It doesn't matter which breed or color of mouse you choose; they all make fine pets. A cinnamon satin and a cinnamon are pictured.

With some adult supervision, mice make good pets for children. Before you buy mice for your child, be sure you are willing to take over their care if your child loses interest.

Young mice are easier to tame and will most likely live longer than an older mouse. Although mice are weaned from their mother at about three to four weeks of age, they should not be moved to a new home until they are at least five weeks old. Recently weaned babies are easily stressed and more susceptible to illness. Some pets stores will know the age of the mice you are considering buying. Five to eight weeks is the best age for a new pet mouse, at which time they are about two to three inches long. Other criteria can be used to determine a mouse's age if the store does not know. A mouse that is too young will have a head that looks too large for its body, his fur may not be smooth and glossy, and he will often move by playful hops instead of walking.

Although most people will buy their pet mice from a pet store or breeder, there are rescue groups that have mice available for adoption. Most of the groups are not specifically mice rescue, but rather specialize in small mammals (sometimes referred to as "small and furry" rescue groups).

Mice and Children

Although having a pet is one of the pleasures of childhood, parents cannot expect a young child to be solely responsible for any pet, regardless of its size. To a varying extent, a parent must participate in the care of a child's pet. Such assistance may be driving to the pet store to buy food or reminding the child to feed the pet or clean the cage. Since young children cannot be expected to care for their pet without some supervision, it helps if a parent is enthusiastic about the pet. Unsupportive parents can make it more difficult for children to care for their pets. Parents can encourage their child to care for the pet simply by showing an interest in the animal.

Children like to play with their pets. If a small pet struggles while being held, some children squeeze harder instead of relaxing their grip. Sometimes this rough handling can frighten a mouse and cause him to bite. Parents can help reduce the risk of a bite by showing their child how to properly hold the mouse and instructing the child on what to do should the mouse begin to wiggle. For example, if the mouse no longer wants to be held, he should be returned to his cage. A parent may have to help take the mouse out of his cage for the child to visit with, or the parent may have to show the child how to open the cage and let the mouse come on his own instead of pulling him from his home. Very young children always need to be supervised when they are playing with a mouse or with any other small pet.

Housing Your Mouse

The cage is the most expensive piece of equipment you will need to purchase for your pet mice. The general rule when buying a cage is to choose the largest cage you can afford. The cage should be a comfortable, roomy home for your mice. A cage that is too small and too confining will become smelly and dirty more quickly. Also, since mice may become grouchy without enough space, they may start fighting. Giving your mice plenty of room to play and explore will make them more interesting and healthy.

Choosing a Cage
Pet stores offer many suitable options for housing your mice.

Mice can be housed in glass aquariums or plastic or wire-frame cages. An ideal cage size for a pair of mice is 20 inches long by 12 inches wide by 10 inches high. The rectangular plastic enclosures with snap-on lids, sometimes called small animal habitats, can be used to house a pair of mice as long as it large enough. These habitats are most suitable to use as carrying cages to take your mice home from the pet store or to the veterinarian. They also provide a secure place to keep your mice while you are cleaning their cage. Be careful with these plastic habitats—they can break if they are dropped.

The cage you choose should be large enough to allow your mice to have space for separate eating, sleeping, and toileting areas. Most manufacturers label their cages for specific kinds of small pets. In general, those labeled for mice, hamsters, gerbils, and rats will make suitable homes for your mice.

Glass Aquarium Cages

A five- or ten-gallon glass aquarium with a secure wire-screen cover will provide a good home for a pair of mice and give the owner a nice all-around view. The aquarium always has to be covered because mice can easily jump out of it. Pet stores sell wire screens with latches to secure to the top of the aquarium just for this purpose. Because the entire top lifts off the aquarium cage, you can readily have access to your pet mice. An aquarium will keep the area around your mice's home tidy since shaving and other debris cannot spill out of the cage, as happens with wire-framed cages. However, the glass sides must be kept clean to prevent them from becoming difficult to see through.

Keep in mind that although glass aquariums and plastic habitats are beneficial because they are not drafty, they also are not well ventilated. Poor ventilation and lax cleaning habits can cause ammonia gas from the urine of the mice to build up to uncomfortable levels. This can irritate the mice's respiratory system.

Plastic critter cages and glass aquaria can be used to house mice, but the lack of ventilation makes them less than ideal.

For your pets' health, you must be vigilant in keeping these types of cages clean. If you think you might be neglectful in cage-cleaning chores, buy a wire-frame cage. Also, aquariums are heavier than wire-frame cages, making them more difficult for a child to move and clean.

Wire-frame Cages

Wire-frame cages made of galvanized steel have good ventilation and offer a good view of your mice. Although they do provide good ventilation, they also have the potential to be drafty. Mice like to climb and wire cages provide them with plenty of opportunity, especially cages that are two or three stories. Plain or colored metal cages are available. Colored cages are often more attractive and can be color-coordinated to match a room. A good-quality wire-frame cage should have a snap-off or slide-out tray for easy cleaning.

Make sure that there is a solid portion of the floor for your mice to sit and stand on. Constantly standing on the wire can make your pet's feet sore. Also, the metal wire can sometimes trap a mouse's foot. To add to your mice's comfort, you can place a small square of

Wire cages provide your mice with good ventilation and plenty of surfaces for climbing. Additionally, it is easy for you to attach toys and wheels to the wires.

non-chewable material, such as a square of plastic, on the bottom of the cage.

If the cage has a snap-off bottom tray, check the tension on the springs before buying it. Some springs are very tight and can be difficult for a child to undo to clean the cage. The cage should have a large door opening to allow you to easily reach inside the cage and take your mouse out. Make sure that the door has no sharp edges and that the door latches securely. The best cages have both a door and a removable top or side to provide easy access to the cage's interior. A handle can make moving the cage easier.

The space between the bars on the cage should be no more than one-quarter to one-half an inch apart to prevent your mice from escaping. This means that you cannot buy a larger cage designed for rabbits, ferrets, or guinea pigs since the space between the bars is too wide. If your mouse is not yet fully grown and can squeeze his head through the cage bars (the rest of his body will undoubtedly follow), temporarily attach a finer wire mesh to the cage until he has grown too big to escape. Such mesh is available at hardware stores.

No Wood

Metal cages do have some drawbacks. Over time, the mice's urine can corrode the metal pan that fits beneath the cage. You can help prevent this problem by cleaning the toileting area every few days. Plastic trays will not corrode from urine, but some mice will chew on the plastic if they can reach it.

High sides on the bottom tray will help catch bedding and other debris that your mice will kick out during their normal activities. Other options for containing the material that spills out are to place the cage on top of newspaper that extends several inches beyond the cage's diameter or to place the cage inside a kitty litter pan.

Other Types of Cages

Colorful plastic housing with connecting tubes allows you to expand your mice's cage into a playground. Like aquariums, however, this type of housing is not as well ventilated as wire cages. Tube housing can also become smelly and difficult to see through if it is not cleaned

A sturdy water bottle is an essential piece of equipment for keeping mice.

Aspen and pine shavings make good bedding materials for mice. You can also use bedding made from recycled paper.

often enough. Some mice can gnaw through the plastic tubes and escape. If you decide to use tube housing for your mice, be sure to choose a large cage with maximum ventilation and a door that is large enough for you to reach in and easily take out your pets.

Bedding

No mater what type of housing you choose, your mice need bedding in their cage. Bedding is used to absorb moisture (from urine and water that may leak from the bottle), reduce odors, and provide a warm, dry place for you mice to sleep. Pet stores carry a variety of small animal bedding that is suitable for mice, including wood shavings such as pine and aspen or more sophisticated bedding made from recycled paper or wood pulp that are designed to help control or eliminate odor. The latter types are more expensive, but they can make it more pleasurable to own mice since their home is less likely to smell unpleasant between cleanings. Bedding made from recycled paper contains no harmful inks, dyes, or significant levels of heavy metals. Whatever bedding you choose, you need only a few inches. Wire flooring in a cage should be completely covered.

Bedding is an important part of your mice's environment and it can affect their health. Ideally, bedding for mice should be dust-free. Dusty bedding can irritate a mouse's respiratory system or aggravate an existing respiratory ailment. In general, paper pulp and recycled paper products tend to be lower in dust compared with wood shavings.

The Cedar Shavings Controversy

Shavings made from softwoods, including pine and cedar, are still the most common type of bedding for mice and other small pets. These beddings have been popular because they are relatively inexpensive and are often fragrant smelling, particularly cedar shavings. However, cedar shavings have been implicated as both causing and aggravating respiratory problems in small animals. In addition, they are known to affect liver function in mice and rats. Although not all experts agree that cedar shavings present a risk to small pets, a growing body of evidence seems to support hobbyists' contentions that cedar shavings can be unhealthy for small animals. Therefore, cedar shavings are not recommended for you mice.

Cage Accessories

Your mice will need several cage accessories, such a food dishes, a hanging water bottle, a nest box, and toys. You can find a wide array of mouse accessories at your local pet shop.

Nests and Pet Stores

Keep in mind that many pet stores do not provide nest boxes for their small pets because they want to make them easier for customers to see. Because the animals are only in the store for a brief period of time, no harm is done.

Paper towel and toilet paper tubes make inexpensive mouse toys. Mice enjoy running through and gnawing on the tubes.

Food Dishes

If you have a metal cage, you can attach the dish to the side to prevent your mice from tipping it over and spilling the contents. If you use a freestanding dish, make sure it is heavy enough that your mice cannot tip it over. Pet stores sell a variety of colorful ceramic dishes that are too heavy for a mouse to move. Mice are not always fastidious and some mice will go to the bathroom in their food dish. Because of this tendency, choose a dish that's too small for you mouse to stand in.

Water Bottle

Provide your mice with fresh water using a gravity-fed water bottle sold at pet stores. Water bottles sold for hamsters are a good size to use with mice. A special holder, also available at pet stores, can be used to hang the water bottle in an aquarium. Do not use an open dish to provide water for your mice. Mice will fill an open container of water with their bedding and droppings, making the water unsanitary and unsuitable for drinking. The increased moisture from a spilled dish of water can also create an unhealthy, damp

Nest Materials

Give your mice unscented tissue paper or paper towels to shred into nesting material. Shredding paper into a nest is a favorite activity among mice. Pet stores also sell nesting material that you can use. However, do not buy artificial fiber bedding sold for birds and hamsters. The small fibers can wrap around a mouse's feet, causing loss of the limb, and sometimes mice eat the material and cannot pass it out of their system.

environment, especially in an aquarium-type cage. The bottle should be placed away from the food dish and the nest box in case it leaks. The bottle's water tube should be at comfortable height for your mice to reach up and drink from, but it should not be so low to the cage floor that the bedding could come in contact with the tube and cause water the bottle to leak.

Nesting Box

Your mice need a nesting box for sleeping and security. This "bedroom" gives your mice a safe hiding place to retreat from loud

Many mouse nests sold in pet stores are made of safe and natural materials, such as sisal, jute, and coconut shells.

Cardboard Toys

Give your mice the cardboard rolls from empty toilet paper or paper towels. You can partially bury these tubes under your pets' bedding and create a system of tunnels for them to explore. Be creative and connect multiple rolls and make multiple entrances and exits. Cardboard egg cartons also provide entertaining play for mice.

noises and any disturbing activity outside their cage. You can buy a nest box at a pet store. A variety of types are sold, including ones that are made to satisfy a small animals natural instinct to chew, such as fruit-flavored cardboard tunnels, huts made from natural plant fibers, and wooden blocks that a pet can hollow out. Other kinds are less destructible and are made of ceramic or hard plastic. You can also make a make a nest box from an old cereal box or cardboard milk carton. Once the box becomes chewed up or smelly, you just replace it.

Toys

Give your mice toys designed for hamsters, such as wooden chew sticks, tunnels, and ladders. Wood chews keep mice busy and active and provide a hard surface on which they can gnaw, which helps

Natural fiber ropes make fun toys for your mice. You can string them from one side of the cage to another to make a rope bridge.

A mouse-sized wooden jungle gym will provide you and your mice with hours of fun. You can use the ones that are made for parrots and sold in many pet stores.

keep their teeth in good shape. Wooden objects, however, absorb urine and other odors and need to be replaced when they are old and smelly. If your mice are housed in an aquarium, you can increase the area available to your mice by adding ladders and platforms.

Mice will enjoy playing with almost anything you put in their cage. The greater the variety of toys, the more fun your mice will have and the more fun they will be to watch. Exercise wheels are wonderful for mice—they really enjoy running on them. Freestanding wheels made of either plastic or metal are sold for use in aquariums or wire cages. The wheel should be big enough to allow your mice to run in it without being cramped or hunched. Make sure to get a solid wheel instead of one with spokes because a mouse can get his tail trapped between the spokes. Mice are agile climbers. A network of ropes strung through the cage will provide hours of play for you mice. It is best to rotate toys through the cage, never leaving a toy in so long that the mice become bored with their environment.

Beware the Gnawing

Mice are enthusiastic gnawers. Do not leave any items such as clothing or papers on or near you pets' cage because anything that can be pulled into the cage will be chewed and destroyed.

Where to Keep the Cage

Your mice should be part of your family. Place their cage in a location where they can be watched and enjoyed. Make the cage a pleasant part of the room. Place the cage on a dresser or table with some attractive fabric underneath it. The floor is not an ideal location because the temperature near the floor is often cooler than on a dresser to table. On top of a high shelf is also not ideal since it will be too high for you to enjoy your mice. Make sure that the cage is in a stable area where it cannot be knocked down

Most of the products sold for hamsters and gerbils will be safe for your mice.

Cleaning Tips

Instead of feeling overwhelmed with the weekly task of cleaning and thus postponing it, try using a kitty litter scoop to quickly remove and replace some of the soiled bedding. Doing so can allow the cage to remain sanitary an extra day or two before you undertake a more meticulous cleaning. Another way to make cage cleaning easier is to buy large quantities of bedding so you always have some around for a quick change.

Do not place the cage near a heating or air conditioning vent, a drafty window, or in direct sunlight. Mice are susceptible to overheating, chills, and drafts. Mice can tolerate a house's normal variations in room light, temperature, and humidity. Do not place your mice's cage next to a lamp or overhead light. Mice do not like bright lights, and strong lights can actually damage an albino mouse's pink eyes. Room temperatures between 65 to 85 degrees Fahrenheit with humidity between 30 to 70 percent all provide satisfactory living conditions for you mice.

You should never keep your mice in the garage. Not only is it an unhealthy environment due to automobile exhaust, but the temperature is also more extreme and variable, and your mice are more likely to be neglected.

Your mice's cage should be placed out of the direct view of the family cat and dog. Your mice will become nervous if a dog or cat constantly sniffs and stares at them. Also, mice are sensitive to the ultrasonic sounds produced by televisions and computers. Therefore, do not place your mice's home near televisions or computers.

Cleaning the Cage

A clean cage plays an important role in keeping your mice healthy.

Odor Control

The ammonia vapors from urine that develop in your pets' cage can make owning mice less than pleasant. The harsh smell is also uncomfortable for the mice. Ammonia is a severe irritant and is detrimental to the health of mice. It affects the mucous membranes of their eyes and respiratory tract. The health of mice can decline if they are regularly exposed to ammonia vapors, and it can make mice more susceptible to opportunistic infections. Mice housed on dirty, moist bedding are most susceptible to these effects, as are mice housed in aquariums that are cleaned infrequently.

The development of innovative bedding products has been spurred by the quest to control or eliminate odor. Scientifically developed bedding products made from a variety of materials, such as recycled paper, do not just mask odor; they are designed to reduce odor by controlling the formation of ammonia. Such beddings promote a healthier environment for mice compared with traditional wood shavings and are highly recommended. If your mice are housed in an aquarium, if you are neglectful in cage cleaning, or if family members object to your pets because they smell, use innovative, odor-controlling bedding.

Plan on cleaning the cage once or twice a week. The more mice kept in a cage, especially in a cage that is relatively small, the more often the cage will need to be cleaned. If, however, your pair of mice live in a very large cage, such as a twenty-gallon aquarium, then it is reasonable to consider cleaning the cage less often than twice a week.

Among pet hobbyists, mice are known for having a strong "mousy" odor, especially the males. A mouse's small, hard droppings do not smell bad, but the urine can develop a pungent ammonia smell. Ammonia is a severe irritant is detrimental to the health of mice.

How to Clean the Cage

To clean your mice's cage, completely change the bedding in the cage and replace it with fresh, clean bedding. In between cleanings, you can do a partial cage change. Other types of small pets, such as gerbils and rats, will establish a toilet area in their cage, which makes cage cleaning easier. Some mice will designate a corner of their cage for a bathroom, but others will go everywhere. Try placing the food dish, water bottle, and nest box at one end of the cage. This will help your mice establish a bathroom area away from their sleeping and eating areas. If you mice do use a corner of the cage for a bathroom area, the bedding in this area can be replaced every few days or so. Doing so will help reduce odor and keep the cage cleaner and more sanitary.

Each week, replace the nesting material in the nest box. Less often, you will need to wash or replace some of your mice's toys and their nest box when they become chewed or tattered. Sometimes these objects absorb urine odors. Replacing them, rather than washing them, will greatly reduce any pungent smell.

A spare cage will come in handy when you are cleaning your mice's cage. It is much easier to clean the cage without the mice in it.

Where's My Smell?

Some mice become upset and frantically run around their home after it has been cleaned. While pet owners find the clean cage refreshing, mice are not often as enthusiastic. They like something with their scent on it and will often become quite busy marking their home again so that is smells better to them. Partial cage cleanings, such as replacing some but not all of your mice's bedding and nesting material, and not washing all of your pets' toys can satisfy your pets' need for something familiar.

Once a month, do a thorough cleaning. Wash the cage with hot, soapy water. Be sure to rinse and dry it thoroughly. If necessary, disinfect the cage with a bleach solution, consisting of one tablespoon of bleach for each gallon of cold water. Wash the water bottle, food dish, and any plastic toys. Wood toys can eventually splinter if washed in water, so scraping them clean with a file is effective. Scrape or file any grime that may have accumulated on the bars of a wire cage.

You will need to place your mice in a secure container, such as a plastic carrying case (small animal habitat) while you clean their home. Some mice owners place their pets in their nest box in the bathtub during cage cleaning. The nest box provides a secure hiding place and the slippery sides of the bathtub are usually too steep for mice to climb or jump out.

Feeding Your Mouse

Feeding your pet mice a healthy diet is easy because a variety of commercial foods are sold for mice at pet stores, usually in packages labeled for hamsters, gerbils, and mice. The dietary requirements for all rodents are similar, and food sold for these pets will provide an adequate diet for mice. Mice eat grains, seeds, fruits, berries, and nuts. Some mice will enjoy eating an occasional invertebrate, such as live mealworms, which you can also buy at pet stores.

Mice are fun to feed because they are adventurous and will eat practically anything you offer them, even foods that are not

Use a sturdy plastic or ceramic food bowl that will hold up to gnawing by your mice.

good for them, such as cookies and candy. It is up to you to provide your mice with a balanced and nutritious diet.

Nutrition is a key factor in promoting good health and a long life. A balanced diet for mice includes the appropriate amount of protein, carbohydrate, fat, vitamins, and minerals. All of these nutrients interact in the building, maintenance, and functioning of

Fats and Carbs

Fats are a significant source of calories and energy. A good diet for mice should contain approximately five percent fat. Fats make up part of the structure of every cell and are necessary for absorption of fat-soluble vitamins A, D, and E. Fats herp to prevent and alleviate skin problems. A deficiency of fat can show up as scaly skin or rough, thin hair.

Carbohydrates are used as a source of energy. Your mice will easily get enough carbohydrates with a diet based on seeds and grains. Most seeds and grains are at least 50 percent carbohydrates.

Supplements

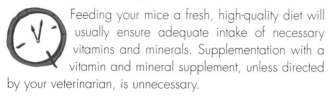

Feeding your mice a fresh, high-quality diet will usually ensure adequate intake of necessary vitamins and minerals. Supplementation with a vitamin and mineral supplement, unless directed by your veterinarian, is unnecessary.

mouse's body. The amount of protein your mice need is influenced by several physiological factors, including age. Mice need less protein when they are adults than they do when they are growing or pregnant or nursing a litter. A good diet for a normal pet mouse should contain between 20 and 24 percent protein.

Vitamins

Vitamins are necessary as catalysts for chemical reactions n the body. The vitamins that mice need in their diet are different than those needed by humans. For example, mice can make their own vitamin C, while humans must get it from an external source, such as oranges. Several vitamins, including many of the B vitamins, are synthesized in mice by intestinal bacteria. These vitamins are available to mice by means of coprophagy, which is when an animal eats special droppings that contain the vitamins synthesized by the bacteria. Mice typically engage in this behavior at night or early in the morning, when you are not likely to observe them. If you do see your mice engaged in such behavior, do not be concerned, just leave them alone. Coprophagy is necessary for their good health.

Freshness

It is important that the food you feed your mice is fresh. Food that is old can become stale and lose some of its nutritional value. Packaged foods should be fresh and sweet smelling, not rancid or dusty. Do not buy a large amount of food because it will take too long to use all of it. Some manufacturers stamp a date on the food bags and recommend that the food be used within one year of that date.

Proper storage of your mice's food is essential. It should be stored in a cool, dry environment. Because sunlight, heat, and time will degrade the vitamins, keep your mice's food in an airtight container, such as a glass jar with a lid, or be sure to completely close self-sealing packaging.

Suggested Diets

Feed your mice one of the rodent mixes sold at pet stores for mice, gerbils, and hamsters. These mixes contain seeds, grains, nuts, alfalfa pellets, and, sometimes, various types of kibble. Avoid food that is mostly sunflower seeds or nuts because such a diet will cause your mice to become overweight.

Mice enjoy picking through their food and eating their favorite items first. Since a nutritional analysis is based on the consumption of the entire mix of ingredients, a selective eater may not be getting a complete, nutritious diet. Over time, this "selective feeding" can cause inadequate nutrition and obesity. While it is reasonable to

Mice enjoy seeds of all types, and seeds are healthy treats for your mice. Do not use seeds intended for gardening, as they are usually treated with fungicides, which may harm your mice.

Mice will usually run through, sit in, and sometimes urinate in the food bowl. Because of this, clean out the food bowl daily.

expect your mice to dislike some of the items in their food, consistently refusing to eat more than half of a food's ingredients is not healthy.

Some mice breeders prefer to feed their mice only nutritionally complete laboratory blocks or pellets specifically made for mice and other rodents (also called pelleted rodent rations). The breeder may also offer these pellets in addition to a rodent mix. The pellets contain a balance of all the nutrients your mice need. They are convenient and easy to feed. Because the pellets are blended, a mouse cannot pick out only one ingredient; therefore, he will consume adequate nutrients. Not all pet stores carry these laboratory blocks, so you may have to ask them to special order them.

How Much to Feed

Your mice should always have food in their dish. Even though they are primarily nocturnal, they will still nibble on food during the day. If your mice's dish is empty, increase the amount of food you give.

Hand-Feeding

If your pets are housed in a wire cage, do not feed them through the cage bars. Otherwise, anything (including a finger) that is poked through the cage bars might get nipped. Always open the cage door to offer a treat. In addition, wash your hands before handling your mice in case any food smells on your hands entice your mice to nip.

Most mice will not overeat. Your mice should feel solid and sleek; they should not have large, bulging bellies. The amount your mice eat will vary depending on what type of food you feed, Typically, mice eat less of the laboratory blocks than they do of the rodent mixes.

When to Feed

It is best to feed your mice that same amount of food at the same time everyday, such as after school or work, or even when you have your own dinner. Since mice are nocturnal, you should feed your

Small portions of fresh vegetables make healthy snacks for your mice. Mice often enjoy the leaves of carrots as well as the carrots themselves.

Quick & Easy Mouse Care

mice in the evening rather than in the morning. Each day you will need to discard the old food in their dish and add fresh food. Some mice store food in a corner of their cage (often under their bedding). Check on their storerooms every once in awhile and discard any food that is damp or moldy.

Food and Activity Levels

You need to feed enough food to meet your mice's energy requirements. The amount will vary according to your mice's age, gender, and activity level. Young, growing mice need to eat more food per gram of body weight than adult mice do. Male mice need to eat more than females since they are larger. Pregnant or nursing mice, however, need more food. Mice who run around and play outside their cage will require more food than mice who just sit in their cage with little to do. Unless you weigh the amount of food you give your mice, you are unlikely to notice these differences because they are very small.

Treats

In addition to your mice's regular diet of grains, seeds, and laboratory blocks, you can offer your mice small amounts of fresh fruit and vegetables, which they love. Mice can be given daily treats of small pieces of fruits and vegetables that have been thoroughly

Unhealthy Treats

While it can be fun to offer your mice new types of food and see if they enjoy them, not all foods are good for mice. Do not feed your mice spoiled people food or junk food of any type. Although mice will greedily eat potato chips and eagerly look for more, potato chips, cookies, candy and other snack foods are not healthy for your mice. Also avoid feeding high-protein, high-fat foods such as dry cat food and the seed and nut mixes sold for parrots and cockatiels.

Compressed alfalfa and timothy bales are sold at many pet stores. Mice enjoy gnawing on them, and this helps wear down their teeth.

washed and dried. The size of your mice's front paws is a reasonable guide when deciding the size of a fresh food item to offer. A mouse should be able to hold the piece of fruit or vegetable between his front paws. Leafy greens should be no more than about one inch by one inch in size. By using these conservative estimates on the amount, you mice are less likely to experience problems, such as diarrhea. Offer your mice only one or two fresh items a day.

Mice enjoy eating hard fruits and vegetables, such as apples and carrots, which are less likely to spoil compared with soft, moist foods like berries and cucumbers. Mice who regularly eat fresh foods are less likely to experience digestive upset than mice who rarely fed such items.

Pet stores sell a variety of tasty treats for mice and other small rodents. But remember, moderation is the key when feeding for your mice treats. Your mice should not eat so many treats that they have no appetite for their regular food. Other treats to try offering your mice include dry, unsweetened cereals, pretzels, crackers, stale (not moldy) bread, hard uncooked noodles, uncooked rice, and uncooked hot cereals (for example, cracked four-grain rice). Many mice love dog biscuits, but be cautious when offering your dog's regular kibble because some brands are high in fat. These treats and the hard food in your mice's regular diet will help to keep their teeth trim.

Live Food

Some mice enjoy eating live moths, mealworms, and crickets. Both crickets and mealworms are sold at pet stores as food for reptiles. It is fascinating to watch a mouse pounce on a mealworm or chase after and catch a cricket to eat. A mouse will turn a mealworm or cricket in his front paws so that he eats the head first before eating the rest of the insect. Not all mice will eat live food; some mice become frightened and want nothing to do with the insect. While some mice owners enjoy watching their pet eat live food, other owners are squeamish. Live food is not necessary, so don't worry if it is not something you want to indulge your mice in. If you do feel

Plain cooked grains are another healthy treat that mice enjoy. Remove fresh foods after a few hours to prevent your mice from eating spoiled foods.

the need to feed your mice live food, make sure you only do so as a treat every few days.

Water

Your mice should always have fresh water available. The amount of water mice drink each day depends on the moisture in their food, so if you give your mice small amounts of fresh fruit and vegetable, they will drink less water. Monitor how much water your mice are drinking. If the amount of water in the bottle does not seem to decrease over a day or so, check the bottle to make sure that the metal spout is not clogged with bedding.

Ideally, your mice's water should be changed daily. Most pet owners, however, do not find this practical or convenient. At the very least, completely change the water in the bottle at least once a week. It might be necessary to change the water more often if you have more than two mice in the cage. Select a water bottle that is large enough that your mice do not run out of water. The standard hamster bottle provides sufficient water to last two mice for most of the week.

It is important to give the water bottle a good cleaning at least once a week. Even if the bottle looks clean, it is probably slimy on the inside and contaminated with bacteria and other harmful pathogens. Use a slender bristle brush to clean the slimy reside that will coat the bottle. Because some mice nibble the metal spout, check to be sure that there are no jagged edges that could cut your mice. If there are, you will need to replace the water bottle.

Quick & Easy Mouse Care

Taming and Handling Your Mouse

A tame mouse will let you hold him and pick him up without becoming frightened. The more time you spend holding and playing with your mouse, the more quickly he will learn to trust you and become tame. The first stage in fully taming your mouse is getting him used to a regular routine and, more important, to you. Mice have an excellent sense of smell and can quickly identify their owners in this way.

It is best to begin your taming sessions in the early evening, when your mice are naturally awake. If your mice are sleeping when you want to play with them, call their names, tap on the nest box, and allow them a few minutes to wake up before you visit. If you startle or grab your mice, they might bite you. Do not force your mice to come out of their nest box when they would clearly rather sleep.

Some mice are very jumpy and active. If your mouse exhibits such behavior, it is best to start taming him by keeping your hand inside their cage, rather than taking him out. Let your mouse sniff and crawl on your hand. Place a food treat in the palm of your hand to encourage him to climb on your hands. Do not make sudden movements with your hands. If your mouse seems confident, try using a finger to pet him along his side or behind his ear. Even a brief stroke will work. Continue to slowly pet your mouse within his cage while talking softly to him so he can get used to your voice. Eventually your mouse will climb on to your hands. He might even climb out of the cage onto your arm. Replace your mouse in his home before he gets too far up your arm.

Holding Your Mouse

You can use one of several methods to pick up a mouse: (1) scoop him up into your hands; (2) pick him up by his tail; or (3) scoop

Mice are most comfortable when allowed to climb on your hand or arm rather than being picked up.

Quick & Easy Mouse Care

Some mice will become used to riding in your pocket; they may even fall asleep in there. Remember that your mouse is in your pocket before going outside or bending over.

Taming and Handling Your Mouse

him up in a small container. The preferred method is to let him climb onto your hand or to scoop him up under his belly. A mouse can be frightened when a hand descends down over his back, so always put your hand in the cage with your palm up, then move it toward the mouse. Do not turn him over on his back and expose his belly. This posture will make him feel vulnerable and he will struggle frantically to right himself. Keep in mind that a normally docile mouse may bite when he is frightened.

You can pick up your mouse by the base or middle of his tail, but you must be extremely gentle and you must immediately allow him to rest his body on your other hand or arm. Do not pick your mouse up by the end of his tail. Doing such will hurt your mouse (the tail may "skin," which is extremely painful) and he can turn and bite you. This will probably cause you to drop him, which could fracture his spine.

Do not hold your mouse by his tail for longer than necessary because he will struggle in an attempt to get away. Instead, let him

You may be able to coax an escaped mouse to come to you with a favorite treat. You can also try putting the nest box on the floor and checking it periodically.

Mice will explore any holes and crevices they can fit into, so make sure their play areas are safe.

rest in one hand and use the other hand to block or control his movements.

Mice do not like being scooped up in a container because containers usually have smooth sides and they have nothing to hold on to. Nonetheless, this method may be useful in an emergency. Be sure that the container you use will fit easily inside the cage. Do not chase your mouse around the cage with the container. Instead, place it on the cage floor and coax your mouse into it. Cover the top of the container with one hand to prevent your mouse from leaping out.

Mice are nimble. Until your mouse is calm and tame, always use two hands to hold him. Loud noises and sudden movements (your own or those caused by another person or pet) could scare your mouse and cause him to jump out of your hands. Use one hand to hold your mouse and lightly cup your other hand over his back or in front of his face. Keep your mouse against your body for greater security. It is also a good idea to sit on the floor when first teaching a mouse to be held. That way, if he does jump, the distance is much less than if you were standing or sitting on a chair.

New Mouse = New Cage

A new cage is an unanticipated cost to purchasing a new mouse friend for your original pet. It is important that the cage or cages you use for the introduction be new. Your original mouse will resent any newcomer's intrusion into his territory. He will be aggressive in defense of his home, and the chances of a successful introduction will be reduced.

Playtime

Mice are fun to watch while they play in their cage. However, most mice owners want to take their pets out of their cage to play. Doing so can be fun and beneficial because the more you play with your mice, the friendlier they will be. While other types of pets, such as rats, rabbits, and gerbils, can be allowed to safely explore and play in a room, mice are too small for such an activity. The chances of their escaping and becoming lost are too great. Instead, think of yourself as their playground—let them play on your while you sit on a bed or a chair. Do not leave your mice unsupervised. They can quickly disappear into small nooks and crannies, and they will be very hard to find.

Other options for play outside of the cage include large plastic enclosures made especially for small pets that you can set up much like a child's playpen, a high-sided (at least 15 inches) plastic swimming pool, or a parrot play-stand. Place bedding, nest boxes, and toys in the playgrounds. Make sure that any enclosure you use is escape-proof. Plastic run-about-balls are another option. Be sure to choose the smaller, mouse-sized ball. Only one mouse at a time can be placed in a ball. Always supervise your mouse when you use a run-about-ball. Stairs and other pets are potential hazards. Some of the balls are designed to move on a racetrack, which helps confine your mouse's movements to a safe place.

Make playtime fun for you and your mice; give them plenty of things to do and new places to explore.

Taming and Handling Your Mouse

An Escapee

Should your mouse escape from his home, place the cage on the floor next to a wall. Do not leave the door open since your other mice will join the wanderer. Instead, provide the remaining mice with a new nest box and take the old nest box and the nesting material and place it on the floor next to the cage. Quite often, the mouse will return to the cage area and then fall asleep inside his familiar nest box.

Introducing Mice to Each Other

If one of your mice dies and you want to get your remaining mouse a companion, you should follow these steps. Mice are territorial and often do not accept an unfamiliar mouse. Adult mice placed together for the first time will fight, sometimes until death. Remember, you can pair a male and a female, or two females, but not two males. If you had two brothers, do not try to pair your remaining male with another male. Buy a younger mouse to increase the chances of success. Younger mice tend to be more readily accepted than another adult.

Several methods can be use to facilitate the introduction. Place your original mouse in a wire cage, and place the new mouse in another wire cage. Slide the two cages together so the mice can smell one another. Alternatively, you can try dividing a cage or aquarium with a piece of wire mesh. You must be certain to securely place the wire so that the weight of a mouse pressing against it will not cause the mesh to fall. If the mesh gives way, the mice could reach each other and they may fight. The spaces between the wire mesh should be small enough that a mouse cannot push his nose through and bite the other mouse.

Over the next several days, switch the mice several times a day between the cages or sides of the cage. Usually the mice will accept one another within several days. If they fight, you must continue

Let your mice out in a mouse-proofed room for some supervised play each day. Keep a careful eye on them to prevent escapes.

Taming and Handling Your Mouse 51

switching them back and forth for several more days before trying again to house them together. Carefully watch your mice for the first few days they share a home to make sure that they do not fight and that they have accepted one another. Any wounds from bites could indicate that the two mice are not getting along. You can reduce the likelihood of your mice fighting by providing each of them with a nest box.

Quarantine

An important caution about introducing a new mouse to your current mouse is the potential risk of also introducing an illness. Serious hobbyists who breed mice usually quarantine a new arrival from their other mice, even if the newcomer seems healthy. A quarantine period helps prevent the transmission of illness among mice. The new arrival is kept in a cage as far away as possible from the other mice. The quarantine period can last from two to four weeks. During that time, the new mouse's health is monitored. Assuming the newcomer shows no signs of ill health, he can be moved into the area containing the other mice when the isolation period is over.

Mouse Health Care

Knowing your mouse's normal behavior will help you recognize when he is sick. Experienced pet owners and breeders are adept at recognizing when a pet is sick. As you gain experience with your mice, especially if you develop a long-term interest, you will also become more proficient. Sick mice generally present a similar range of symptoms. Obvious signs of illness include discharge from the eyes or nose, sudden change in behavior, lethargy, reduced appetite, and failure to groom. Signs of illness that are more difficult to detect include rough fur, hunched posture, and weight loss. You should pay particularly close attention if your mouse is sensitive when touched on a certain part of his body—this could indicate an injury from being squeezed or dropped. Any of these symptoms suggest that something might be wrong with your mouse and that a visit to the veterinarian may be necessary.

Act Fast

Most sick mice need to be treated immediately by a veterinarian. This is especially important because pet owners often do not notice symptoms in their mouse until he is very ill. By the time a mouse owner realizes that there is something wrong, the mouse has usually been sick for quite some time. In many such cases, treatment is difficult because the condition usually is advanced by the time of detection. Although some diseases progress rapidly and an affected mouse can die suddenly, early recognition of a sick mouse may mean the difference between life and death. Furthermore, keep in mind that the sicker a mouse is, the more likely he is to be traumatized from the procedures at the veterinarian's office.

Finding a Veterinarian

In order for a mouse to receive the proper treatment, he needs the correct diagnosis. A veterinarian who routinely treats rodents and has a special interest in their care is best qualified and will most likely have the smaller-sized equipment necessary to perform veterinary procedures. In order to locate a veterinarian who is knowledgeable about rodents, inquire at pet stores, critter clubs, and rescue societies.

Don't Play Vet

Home diagnosis of anything but minor problems is fraught with danger. Many of the clinical signs of ill health are the same for a whole range of diseases, but the treatments for them can differ considerably. If the diagnosis is not accurate, then it is not possible to prescribe a course of treatment. Often, microscopy of a blood sample, fecal mater, or a skin scraping is needed. Only your vet can attend to this need and provide the correct diagnosis to your mouse.

Quick & Easy Mouse Care

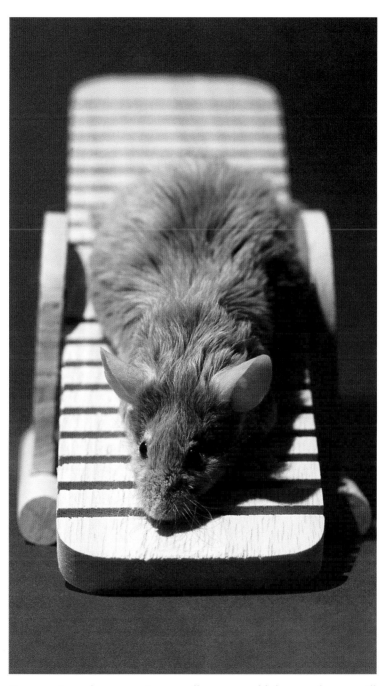

Pay attention to how your mice normally appear and behave, so that you will recognize any changes that could indicate illness.

Mouse Health Care

Changes in the cage location, diet, and light cycle can cause mice stress.

Discuss potential costs with your veterinarian beforehand, so you will have a better idea of how much your mouse's care might cost. Although it may be difficult to put a price on your pet, in some cases, it may be necessary to decide how much you can afford to spend.

Stress

Stress is a catch-all word for a variety of conditions that disturb or interfere with a mouse's normal physiological equilibrium. Because stress often leads to illness, it is frequently mentioned as a detrimental, contributing factor to various diseases. Besides becoming sick, a mouse can exhibit signs of stress in other ways, such as nervousness, lack of appetite, hair loss, or loose droppings.

It is useful for pet owners to be aware of what constitutes stress for their mice. A mouse can experience stress from pain and fear, moving to a new cage, a change in diet, and/or exposure to temperature fluctuations. The trip home for a new pet can be frightening and stressful for a mouse. Once in their new home, some mice settle down right away while others take longer to adjust.

Other stressful situations include loud noises, overcrowding, and harassment by other pets, including other mice. Groups of mice housed together can fight and injure one another. Stress can be a major factor in the development of what otherwise might remain a dormant disease. It is, therefore, wise to minimize the stress in your mice's life.

Causes of Illnesses

The ailments that might affect mice can be classified into five categories: (1) trauma-induced injuries; (2) infectious disease; (3) noninfectious disease; (4) improper husbandry; and (5) problems related to aging. The reason why a mouse becomes sick is often a combination of factors from more than one category. For example, a poorly ventilated cage can create a noxious-smelling environment with high levels of ammonia that can cause an outbreak of a latent respiratory disease. How sick the mouse will become depends on the virulence of the pathogen, the mouse's age and dietary deficiencies, and whether the mouse is already sick with another illness.

Trauma-induced Injuries

A traumatic injury is usually caused when a mouse is dropped, falls, or is squeezed while being held. If a mouse is injured, especially if he appears to be in pain, you should take him the veterinarian immediately. The veterinarian can determine whether the injury can be treated or whether it is kinder to end the mouse's suffering through euthanasia. Occasionally, some trauma injuries (such as an injured toe) get better despite no care. Broken bones are a potential hazard for mice because they can accidentally jump from your hands if something frightens them. Properly holding and playing with your mice can prevent such injuries from happening.

Injuries from fighting among mice can also occur. Fighting mice will typically bite each other on the shoulder, rump, scrotum, and tail. Because infection from bacteria is always possible when a mouse is bitten, clean any bloody injuries with warm water and an antiseptic or hydrogen peroxide. An abscess can develop at the site of a bite wound due to bacterial infection. Watch the wound, and if you detect any prolonged swelling, which could indicate an abscess, take your mouse to the veterinarian.

Infectious Diseases

Infectious diseases can spread from one animal to another and are caused by bacteria, viruses, and protozoans. Sometimes the disease caused by these agents are subclinical, with signs of infection that are difficult to detect. Individual animals also differ in their resistance to infectious organisms. Some exposed animals never display symptoms. However, stress or other bacterial or viral infections can cause an animal to suddenly show symptoms. A single pet is at less risk of acquiring an infectious disease than a pet housed in close proximity to large numbers of other animals of the same species. Infectious diseases are often preventable through good husbandry.

A shaggy coat is normal for the rex breed of mouse. Changes in the fur of a mouse could indicate that he has mites.

Noninfectious Disease and Ailments

Mites

Mice can sometimes be infested with mites, which are external parasites. Some mites are visible to the unaided eye, but others can only be seen under a microscope. Mites usually affect animals and typically do not affect their owners. Symptoms of mite infestation include thinning hair, greasy coat, and scabs. For accurate diagnosis and treatment, your mice must be seen by a veterinarian who will identify the type of mites your mice are infected with and prescribe the appropriate treatment. If you obtained your mice from a clean, reliable source, mites should not be a problem.

Zoonotic Diseases

Parents are sometimes concerned about whether mice can give their children an illness, especially because children often forget to wash their hands after playing with their pets. Zoonotic diseases are diseases that can be transmitted from animals to people. Some pet owners develop allergies, such as a skin rash, to mice dander and urine. The potential for disease transmission is reduced with proper hygiene such as washing your hands after playing with your pets and keeping their cage clean. Purchasing your mice from a clean environment rather than a smelly, dirty one further reduces the chance of a mouse having a zoonotic disease. Fortunately, pet mice rarely carry diseases that can affect people.

Barbering

If you keep more than two mice together in a cage, you may see a condition called barbering. A dominance hierarchy always forms among a group of mice. The dominant mouse bites or chews the muzzle and face of the lower-ranked mice, which results in patches of lost hair and lost whiskers. Removing the dominant mouse—usually the one with no bald areas—will help reduce this behavior. However, sometimes the next most dominant mouse will simply begin barbering the remaining cage occupants.

Tumors

Some tumors are benign, while others are cancerous and will cause the death of an affected mouse. Tumors are seldom seen in young mice. They usually occur in middle-aged and older mice. Mammary tumors are the most frequently seen tumor in mice. When playing with your mouse, you may notice a swelling under the skin, which could be a tumor or an abscess. If your mouse has a lump, you should have it checked by a veterinarian to determine if it is a tumor. Some tumors can grow quite large and will eventually interfere with a mouse's ability to move. A veterinarian can surgically remove a tumor, although the tumor will often recur. It is

Sometimes the dominant mouse in a group will chew off the hair and whiskers of other mice. This is called barbering.

important to have a tumor removed early because large tumors can be more difficult to remove.

Malocclusion

Although not common, the teeth of some mice need veterinary attention due to malocclusion. Malocclusion occurs when a mouse's incisor teeth do not meet properly, either because they are overgrown or are misaligned. A mouse's teeth can fail to meet and wear properly for several reasons. Malocclusion can be inherited, or it can be caused by trauma, infection, or improper diet. For example, the mouse does not regularly eat foods hard enough to wear down his teeth. Hereditary malocclusion is often not detectable in young mice. Even if you inspected the mouse's teeth before you bought him and they appeared normal, the teeth can become misaligned as the mouse grows.

Mice with this condition eventually cannot eat and they lose weight and die without treatment. Many show symptoms often referred to as "slobbers," which are threads of saliva around then mouth and sometimes wiped on the front paws. If you notice your mouse is not eating, you can check his incisors by pulling back his lips. An affected mouse should be taken to a veterinarian who will clip or file the mouse's teeth.

Improper Husbandry

Husbandry is a big word for how a pet is taken care of and includes aspects such as housing, food, and water. A mouse is completely dependant on you to provide the proper environment because mice cannot modify the size, temperature, air circulation, and cleanliness of their home. Providing a spacious, clean cage is one of the most important ways you can keep your mice healthy. Spoiled food and a dirty cage are an invitation for illness. Routine cleaning is the most effective method for preventing disease organisms from becoming established in your mice's home and overpowering their natural resistance to disease. Your mice are most likely to get sick if you become forgetful about cleaning their cage.

Nutrition

If you are feeding your mice a balanced diet, it is unlikely your mice will have nutritional problems. However, if your mice can pick out their favorite bits of food and leave the rest, they may end up with vitamin and mineral deficiencies or become obese. Monitor your mice's eating habits to make sure they are getting a balanced and varied diet.

Like people, mice can have food allergies. Some mice are allergic to peanuts. Symptoms of such an allergy are scabs on the mouse's head and

When kept in the proper conditions and fed a balanced and varied diet, mice are not prone to illnesses.

shoulders due to excessive scratching. A veterinarian can confirm that the scabs are not caused by a mite infestation. Eliminating peanuts from the mouse's diet will eventually result in the complete healing of the scabs.

Problems Related to Aging

As a mouse gets older, you may begin to notice changes in his behavior and body condition due to aging. Symptoms often appear gradually and pet owners sometimes do not notice. However, mice become more prone to illness as they age. Noninfectious ailments such as tumors and cataracts are usually seen in older mice. Depending on their heredity, some old mice become skinny while others have a tendency to gain weight. Old mice also groom themselves less frequently, thus their fur looks less sleek and shiny.

Considering whether to euthanize an old mouse is very painful. Your veterinarian can help you with this decision. The time to discuss this option is when your mouse is no longer able to leave his nest box, must be force fed, or is terminally ill. In some cases, it may be better for a mouse to painlessly be put to sleep rather than be subjected to stressful treatment that may only add a few weeks to his life.

Resources

MAGAZINES

Critters USA
Fancy Publications, Inc.
3 Burroughs
Irvine, CA 92618
Phone: (888) 738-2665
www.fancypubs.com

ORGANIZATIONS

American Rat, Mouse, and Hamster Society
Denise Boyce
8275 Westmore Road #30
San Diego, CA 92126
Phone: (619) 390-2903
Fax: (619) 390-5271
www.altpet.net/rodents/rats/ARMHS.html

American Fancy Rat and Mouse Association
9230 64th Street
Riverside, CA 92509-5924
Phone: (626) 966-0350
E-mail: rattusrat@hotmail.com
www.afrma.com

Australian National Rodent Association
P.O. Box 2079
Toowong
Brisbane, Qld 4066
Australia
E-mail: anraqld@hotmail.com
http://members.tripod.com/anraq/

The London & Southern Counties Mouse & Rat Club
153 Kenilworth Crescent
Enfield, Middlesex
EN1 3RG
England
E-mail: lscmrc@miceandrats.com
www.miceandrats.com

North American Rat & Mouse Club, Intl.
Candy Evans
104 N. Lincoln Ave.
Wenonah, NJ 08090
Phone: (609) 932-1258
E-mail: NARMCI@usa.com
http://narmci.8k.com/index.html

WEB RESOURCES

The National Mouse Club
www.nationalmouseclub.co.uk

Rodentfancy
www.rodentfancy.com

Rodents Are Great
www.the-rag.com

Pet Parade
www.pet-parade.com

Pet Finder
www.petfinder.org

RESCUE AND ADOPTION SERVICES

ASPCA
424 East 92nd Street
New York, NY 10128-6801
Phone: (212) 876-7700
E-mail: information@aspca.org
www.aspca.org

RSPCA
Wilberforce Way
Southwater
Horsham, West Sussex RH13 9RS
Telephone: 0870 3335 999
www.rspca.org.uk

EMERGENCY SERVICES

ASPCA Animal Poison Control Center
Telephone: (888) 426-4435
E-mail: napcc@aspca.org (for non-emergency, general information only)
www.apcc.aspca.org

Index

Photo Credits

Glen S. Axelrod: 12, 24
I. Francais: 1, 19, 31, 51
M. Gilroy: 3, 4, 6, 7, 8, 11, 13, 17, 26,
    28, 34, 40, 41, 43, 44, 45, 46, 47,
    49, 53, 55, 56, 58, 60, 61

Tony David Jones: 15
R. Luedtke: 22,
J. Tyson: 27, 33, 37
M. Walls: 38